Buckingham Palace

OFFICIAL SOUVENIR GUIDE

Contents

Introduction

Buckingham Palace is one of the most readily recognised buildings in the world. Like the Houses of Parliament and the red double-decker bus, it stands as an international symbol of London and, by extension, of the United Kingdom as a whole. However, unlike many of the capital's most famous historic buildings, it is not a museum. The Palace is the working headquarters of the monarchy, where Her Majesty The Queen carries out her official and ceremonial duties as Head of State of the United Kingdom and Head of the Commonwealth. The Queen spends the working week at Buckingham Palace and is normally at Windsor Castle at the weekend. At Christmas and for the month of January, Her Majesty resides at Sandringham, her private estate in Norfolk, and the months of August and September are spent at Balmoral in the Highlands of Scotland. As one of the few working royal palaces remaining in the world, Buckingham Palace has a particular fascination.

The state rooms form the heart of the working palace and occupy the main (west) block, facing the gardens. It is in these rooms that many official functions take place, from large-scale events such as state banquets and investitures, to private audiences with ambassadors and foreign heads of state. Since 1993, the state rooms of Buckingham Palace have been open to the public for two months each summer, and to date this tour has been enjoyed by over six million people from many parts of the world.

This official souvenir guide provides an account of the history of the Palace, and a guide to the state rooms and their use, and to the magnificent works of art on display. Further sources of information are listed inside the back cover.

RIGHT
The Changing of the Guard.

LEFT
The Sovereign's Standard flying during a state visit. If The Queen is in residence, the Standard will be flying on the central flagstaff; otherwise, the Union flag will be seen. On great ceremonial occasions, weather permitting, an especially large Standard is flown.

RIGHT
The Queen meets Olympic medallists Chris Hoy (right) and Rebecca Adlington (centre right) during the Beijing Olympics Team GB reception at Buckingham Palace, 2008.

The Palace is 108 metres wide across the front, 120 metres deep (including the central Quadrangle) and 24 metres tall.

There are 775 rooms, including 19 state rooms, 52 royal and guest bedrooms, 188 staff bedrooms, 92 offices and 78 bathrooms.

There are 760 windows, which are cleaned every six weeks, and 1,514 doors.

The Palace is furnished with more than 20,000 works of art.

More than 30,000 guests, from every part of the country and the Commonwealth, and drawn from all walks of life, attend The Queen's garden parties in July each year.

A further 7,000 come as guests or recipients of honours to the 21 investitures or to the numerous receptions held throughout the year.

The largest event, The Queen's Diplomatic Reception, takes place in early November and is attended by approximately 1,000 members of the Diplomatic Corps.

The highlight of royal entertaining is the state banquet, usually for 170 guests, given by The Queen on the first evening of a state visit by a foreign head of state to the United Kingdom. State banquets are held in the Ballroom, the largest of the state rooms, using magnificent gold plate from the Royal Collection, much of it made for George IV (r.1820–30).

Each week that Parliament is in session, the Prime Minister is received in private audience at Buckingham Palace.

Around 400,000 people visit the Palace during the Summer Opening.

THE WORKING PALACE

RIGHT
The display of the wedding cake of the Duke and Duchess of Cambridge in the Picture Gallery on 29 April 2011.

Some 450 people work in the Palace. In addition to those directly supporting The Queen in the management of her official programme, there are those responsible for the maintenance of the buildings and grounds, for finance, communications, information technology, personnel, fire safety, and the public opening of the official residences. In addition, there are those jobs that are uniquely royal, such as the footmen, pages and yeomen of the pantries (responsible for the china, glass and silver) and those that are nowadays more rare, such as the fendersmith (responsible for cleaning and repairing the metal fenders of the fireplaces,) the pipe major and the two clockmakers, who maintain more than 350 clocks in working order.

The head of the Royal Household is the Lord Chamberlain. Under him are the heads of five departments:

👑 The Private Secretary, who plans The Queen's programme, acting as the channel between The Queen and the Government and dealing with appointments, constitutional and political matters;

👑 The Comptroller of the Lord Chamberlain's Office, who is in charge of ceremonial;

👑 The Keeper of the Privy Purse, who looks after royal finances, property maintenance and personnel;

👑 The Master of the Household – a position dating back to 1539 – who is responsible for the organisation of official entertaining; and

👑 The Director of the Royal Collection, who is responsible for the care and display of works of art and for managing the opening arrangements for the official palaces, the Royal Mews and The Queen's Galleries.

BELOW AND LEFT
Palace staff prepare the state rooms for a variety of official events every week.

Architectural History

The famous façade of Buckingham Palace is less than 100 years old. Its construction in 1913 was one of the most dramatic and efficient building projects ever seen in London, completed in just three months. The East Wing itself had been built for Queen Victoria (r.1837–1901) only in 1847, enclosing what had until then been an open, three-sided forecourt.

The creation of the Palace was begun by the architect John Nash (1752–1835) in 1825, but was interrupted by the death of George IV five years later and not completed until around 1840, in the early years of the reign of Queen Victoria. Nash's starting point was a far less imposing building, Buckingham House, which had been purchased in 1762 by George III (r.1760–1820) as a private residence for his wife, Queen Charlotte (1744–1818).

At that time, Buckingham House stood on the edge of the City of Westminster, at the western end of the Tudor hunting park of St James's.

EARLIER BUILDINGS

The history of the site of Buckingham Palace began more than 100 years before it became a royal house. It was here that in the reign of James I (1603–25) a plantation of mulberries was established under royal patronage for the rearing of silkworms. When the garden was granted by Charles I (r.1625–49) to Lord Aston in 1628, there was already a substantial house standing.

The first documented building work on the site took place in 1633, when Lord Goring, who had purchased it from Aston's son, built 'a fair house and other convenient buildings, and outhouses, and upon other part of it made the ffountaine garden, a Tarris [terrace] walke, a Court Yard, and laundry yard'.

By 1668, the house had become the home of Henry Bennet, Charles II's (r.1660–85)

Secretary of State and later Earl of Arlington. In September 1674, it was entirely consumed by fire with, as diarist John Evelyn recorded, 'exceeding losse of hangings, plate, rare pictures and Cabinets'. Arlington immediately rebuilt, exploiting the newly created axial features of St James's Park, laid out for Charles II. These were the long double avenue along the southern edge of St James's Palace, on the line of the Mall, and the canal extending from Horse Guards to the western edge of St James's Park, itself lined with double avenues.

In 1698, the house was let on a short lease to John Sheffield (1648–1721), 3rd Earl of Mulgrave and Marquess of Normanby, who was created Duke of Buckingham in 1703. A year later, Sheffield acquired the house and demolished it. The new house built by the Duke of Buckingham stood exactly on the site now occupied by Buckingham Palace, and its essential plan and the layout of its forecourt dictated all subsequent rebuilding.

Later, when the house was in the hands of the Duke's illegitimate son, Sir Charles Sheffield, George III's mentor and adviser John, 3rd Earl of Bute, began in 1761 to engineer the purchase of the house for the King. Sheffield was obliged to part with it for £28,000.

This could not have come at a more fortuitous time, for it was in September 1761 that the new King George III welcomed his bride Princess Charlotte of

Mecklenburg-Strelitz to England. The marriage ceremony took place in the Tudor palace of St James's, which, though modernised under Queen Anne (r.1702–7) and George II (r.1727–60), was conspicuously uncomfortable. The acquisition of Buckingham House instantly provided the King with a more appealing alternative; he explained to Lord Bute that it was 'not meant for a palace, but a retreat'. It would become the King and Queen's London residence, while St James's was maintained as the official seat of the court.

RIGHT
Sutton Nichols (*fl.* 1725–55), *Buckingham House in 1731.* Engraving. The best contemporary artists and craftsmen were employed on Buckingham House, including the sculptor John Nost (d.1729), who provided statues of *Apollo, Liberty, Equity, Mercury, Truth* and *Secrecy* for the parapet.

The young George III lost no time in taking possession of his new house. In the spring of 1762, he wrote to Lord Bute:

... there seems to Me but little necessary to make it habitable; as to the Furniture, I would wish to keep nothing but the Picture in the Middle panel of the Japan Room, & the four glasses in the Room, they all having Japan frames ... All I have to recommend is dispatch that I may soon get possession of it ...

Notwithstanding this initial reaction, between 1762 and 1776 the house was transformed, at a cost of £73,000.

Beginning with the exterior, the King ordered the removal of the more ornate baroque features, such as the statues and the

LEFT
Johann Zoffany (1733/4–1810), *Queen Charlotte with her Two Eldest Sons, c.*1765.

BELOW
William Westall (1781–1850), *Buckingham House: the East (Entrance) Front,* 1819. Watercolour.

fountain in the forecourt. The extravagant gates and their railings were swept away in favour of a much simplified, lower arrangement giving an air of informality to the front. In 1775, the house was settled on Queen Charlotte in exchange for Somerset House and, from this time onwards, Buckingham House became known simply as 'the Queen's House'.

The Queen's rooms upstairs were among the most sophisticated of their date in London, while the King's rooms on the ground floor below were markedly simple in comparison. Johann Zoffany's paintings record the family life that George III and Queen Charlotte valued above all other things, and of which the Queen's House was the focus. It was here that all but one of their 15 children were born, and here that they had their nurseries and governesses. Following the deaths of both George III and Queen Charlotte, George IV made clear that there were 'early associations which endear me to the spot'.

BELOW
James Stephanoff (1789–1874), *The Queen's Breakfast Room*, 1818–19. Watercolour.

BELOW
John Nash's proposal model.

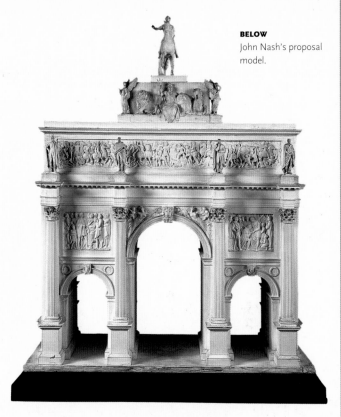

THE MARBLE ARCH

The triumphal arch designed by John Nash for the centre of the forecourt was perhaps inspired by that of Constantine in Rome, but no doubt more directly based on the Arc de Triomphe du Carrousel, which Napoleon's architects had recently erected in a similar position at the Tuileries in Paris. The arch was intended as part of a ceremonial processional approach to the Palace and would be a celebration of recent British naval and military victories, with friezes in honour of the Duke of Wellington and Lord Nelson on each side, and surmounted by a bronze equestrian statue of George IV.

Work on the Marble Arch was halted upon the death of George IV and Parliament's subsequent dismissal of Nash. It remained in place until the reign of Queen Victoria, when the architect Edward Blore (1787–1879) was charged with the design of a wing enclosing the Palace forecourt. Although the Arch was in situ during the construction of Blore's façade, it was clearly at odds with the new addition and was taken down in 1850 and re-erected in its current position at Cumberland Gate, on the north-eastern edge of Hyde Park, in 1852.

13

ARCHITECTURAL HISTORY

GEORGE IV AND BUCKINGHAM PALACE

RIGHT
Sir Thomas Lawrence
(1769–1830), *George IV*,
1821. The Table of the
Grand Commanders, one
of the treasures of the
Royal Collection, can be
seen on the left of the
painting. Today it is in the
Blue Drawing Room
(see page 58).

In 1820, the new King, George IV, had to decide where the official business of privy councils and audiences, and the obligations of the monarchy to entertain large numbers of guests, should take place. His own London residence, Carlton House, halfway along Pall Mall, was not suitable. In the first decades of the century, the balance had already tipped away from St James's Palace and towards the Queen's House. Meanwhile, foreign visitors and journalists remarked with increasing frequency on the fact that in the burgeoning capital city of the greatest power in the world there was no proper royal palace.

In July 1821, responsibility for Buckingham House was given to Nash, who since 1813 had been engaged on the final transformation of the Royal Pavilion at Brighton, becoming in the process a close confidant of the new King. In May 1825, the architect was instructed by the Chancellor of the Exchequer to prepare plans for the expansion and modernisation of Buckingham House.

Nash's design was essentially an enlargement of the plan of Buckingham House. The central block was extended westwards and to the north and south, and the two wings to the east were rebuilt

BELOW
G. Humphrey,
*Guests Arriving for a
Royal Drawing Room at
Buckingham House in
1822.* Engraving.

in much the same style as Nash had deployed on the Regent's Park terraces. The wings enclosed a forecourt, or *cour d'honneur*, that would transform the aspect of the new Palace from St James's Park, which in George III's time had been markedly informal.

When first completed, the wings were a single storey in height, rising to two storeys halfway along and three at their eastern ends. These new features were greeted with a furore of public and official criticism. The outcome was that the wings were rebuilt to the same height as the main block. In the middle of the forecourt, between the two wings, there was to be a triumphal arch.

Despite the controversy, Nash's Buckingham Palace was a masterpiece, exactly answering the need for a palace that reflected Britain's standing in the world, and providing a suitably dignified setting for the Sovereign and court. The ingredients were the advanced, French-inspired Neoclassical design, the quality of the materials and the involvement of outstanding artists and craftsmen.

By the time of the King's death in 1830, the Palace was far from finished. Much of the fitting-out of the state rooms remained to be completed and very little had been done about furniture or the functioning parts – the 'necessary offices' such as the kitchens and laundries – that would make it habitable. No sooner was the King dead than the Prime Minister, the Duke of Wellington (1769–1852), intervened to 'make a Hash of Nash' and to call a halt to further expenditure.

Most of the internal plaster decorations were designed by Thomas Stothard, a versatile painter and book illustrator. Ever since the Elgin Marbles went on display for the first time at the British Museum in 1817, a processional frieze became almost de rigueur for new public buildings. Stothard's genius turned Grecian into Gothic for the distinctly British friezes that he designed for the Throne Room at Buckingham Palace, which represent scenes from the Wars of the Roses. Subjects from British history were also chosen for the friezes on the West Front and the Marble Arch.

RISING COSTS

In 1828 and 1831, the modernisation plans for Buckingham House were examined by Select Committees of Parliament, to which Nash and each of his contractors in turn submitted evidence, while other leading architects and engineers were called to give their opinion on the structural integrity of the building. Following the King's death in 1830, Nash was dismissed by Parliament.

ABOVE
William Heath (1795–1840), John Bull calls Nash to account for his over-expenditure on the Palace, 1829. Engraving.

WILLIAM IV AND THE COMPLETION OF THE PALACE

After Nash was dismissed, Blore was appointed as architect. The new King William IV (r.1830–7), George IV's brother, showed no interest in moving from Clarence House, which Nash had recently built for him within St James's Palace. Indeed, when in 1834 the old Houses of Parliament were destroyed by fire, the King offered the still-incomplete building as a ready-made replacement. The offer was respectfully declined and Parliament voted to allow the 'completing and perfecting' of the Palace for royal use.

Blore's somewhat thankless work involved the completion of the state apartments to Nash's designs and the provision of all the necessary offices.

He extended the east façade at both ends and created a new entrance (the Ambassadors' Entrance) on the southern side, through which those with the privilege of entrée would be admitted to Drawing Rooms and through which summer visitors to the Palace now enter.

The furnishing stage had not been reached at Buckingham Palace during George IV's lifetime. What plans there were had been based on the assumption that Carlton House – which was demolished in 1827 – would contribute the greater part of the pictures and other furnishings, supplemented by some of the pre-existing contents of the Queen's House and by surplus furnishings from Windsor.

ABOVE
Martin Archer Shee (1769–1850), *William IV*, 1833–4.

NEW TECHNOLOGY

Nash was alive to the possibilities afforded by new technology, such as the structural use of cast iron. Not only the principal joists concealed within the structure, but also all the Doric columns of the ground floor were cast in Staffordshire and brought to London by the network of canals. Plate glass for the windows and for the mirrored and glazed doors was available from suppliers in nearby Vauxhall using the latest processes.

For the friezes and external capitals, Nash was able to turn to William Croggon, successor to Mrs Eleanor Coade in the manufacture of artificial stone. Named after its creator, Coade stone was a ceramic substance invented in England in the late eighteenth century, which could be employed as an artificial stone, either

for sculpture or for the decoration of buildings. It was a cost-effective alternative to carved stone and remained ubiquitous in British buildings and gardens until the 1840s, when it was superseded by more modern materials.

RIGHT
The east Quadrangle Front. At the angles of the pediment there originally stood Coade stone figures of Britannia, Commerce and Neptune. National devices appear in the continuous Coade stone frieze of the Quadrangle façades, which incorporates the rose, shamrock and thistle.

QUEEN VICTORIA AND THE 'HEADQUARTERS OF TASTE'

In February 1845 Queen Victoria wrote to the Prime Minister, Sir Robert Peel (1788–1850), about the 'urgent necessity of doing something about Buckingham Palace'. She pointed out:

... the total want of accommodation for our little family, which is fast growing up ... A room capable of containing a larger number of those persons whom the Queen has to invite in the course of the season to balls, concerts etc. is much wanted. Equally so, improved offices and servants' rooms, the want of which puts the departments of the household to great expense yearly.

Blore was again consulted and instructed to prepare plans for a new wing. Brighton Pavilion had been sold in 1846 and the proceeds of the sale (£53,000) were directed towards this new wing. The Board of Works further insisted that the fixtures and fittings removed from Brighton, including chimneypieces, panelling, light fittings and grates, should be incorporated into the interior.

Exotic as they were, it is worth remembering that the main ingredients of the reused Brighton interiors had been designed by Nash only a few years before his work on Buckingham Palace. The redecoration of the original state rooms of the Palace, which Prince Albert (1819–61) had begun before the new East Wing was built, was in some ways far more radical. The Prince was a serious student of Italian Renaissance art and when travelling in Italy in 1839 he had met Ludwig Gruner (1801–62).

ABOVE
William Simpson (1823–99), *The Return of the Guards from the Crimea, Outside Buckingham Palace*, 9 July 1856. Watercolour. By far the most significant element of Blore's design was the central balcony, which was incorporated at Prince Albert's suggestion. From here Queen Victoria saw her troops depart to the Crimean War and welcomed them on their return.

Their work at the Palace began with the redecoration of the Grand Staircase, previously painted a uniform pale ochre shade. In 1846, it was repainted in a complex polychrome scheme best seen in Eugène Lami's watercolour of guests arriving at a ball in 1848 (see pages 2 and 38).

The second part of Queen Victoria's request was finally fulfilled in 1851, when

ABOVE
Sir Edwin Landseer (1803–73), *Queen Victoria and Prince Albert at the Bal Costumé of 12 May 1842*, 1842–6.

LEFT
George Housman Thomas (1824–68), *Buckingham Palace: Queen Victoria and Prince Albert Inspecting Wounded Grenadier Guardsmen*, 20 February 1855. Watercolour.

builder and developer, Thomas Cubitt,
submitted designs for a new ballroom on
the south side of the Palace. Sir James
Pennethorne (1801–71) was appointed as
architect, completing his designs in 1852.
Pennethorne had studied in Paris and Rome
and had served his apprenticeship in Nash's
office during the original construction of
the Palace. He was responsible for many of
the most prominent public buildings
in London, such as the façade of
Burlington House in Piccadilly.

Pennethorne designed two very
large rooms, the Ball and Concert
Room and Ball Supper Room and,
beneath them, fully equipped
kitchens and associated 'offices'. For
the decoration, Prince Albert called
once again on Gruner, whose studies
of Italian mural paintings inspired
the treatment of the rooms. The
decoration of the Ball Supper Room
was remarkably sumptuous,
conceived as the interior of an exotic
tent. As described in the architectural
magazine *The Builder*, the central
dome was:

*... a blue velarium, sown with golden stars, and bordered
by arabesques ... it is painted as if the sky was seen
beyond, between the cords which tie it down at the foot ...*

As first completed, the Ballroom and
Supper Room placed Buckingham Palace in
the avant-garde of decoration in England,
leading the critic of *The Builder* to designate
the Palace as 'Headquarters of Taste'.

These decorations survived for the
remainder of the century. After Prince
Albert's untimely death in 1861, Queen
Victoria declared that nothing for which he
had been responsible should be touched.
During her long absences from the Palace
in the ensuing 40 years, whether at Osborne,
Windsor or Balmoral, the effects of
London's atmosphere – heavily laden with
coal dust and smoke – infiltrated every
corner of the building.

BELOW
Eugenio Agneni
(1832–1910), *The
Children's Fancy Ball Held
in the Ball Supper Room
on 7 April 1859 for the
Sixth Birthday of Prince
Leopold*. Watercolour.

FROM EDWARD VII TO THE PRESENT DAY

With this in mind, King Edward VII's (r.1901–10) decision to redecorate following his accession in 1901 may be better understood. In the Grand Entrance, Marble Hall and Grand Staircase, the Victorian polychrome decorations were replaced with the all-pervading white-and-gold scheme that survives today. It seems that the King was shown proposals for the remodelling of the Ballroom by Frank T. Verity (1864–1937), the official architect of the Lord Chamberlain's Office.

The redecoration was eventually begun in 1906–7. In the Ballroom, the end walls, the organ and the arch enclosing the throne remained as Pennethorne had left them, but otherwise the room was largely repainted in the ubiquitous white and gold. A similar simplifying operation was undertaken in the Ball Supper Room.

If, in carrying out these extensive works to the interior, King Edward might have seemed to be acting hastily to erase his parents' considerable contributions to the appearance of the Palace, he was quick to lend his support and patronage to the Queen Victoria Memorial. Having begun his long career as an assistant on the sculpture of the Albert Memorial in Kensington Gardens, the sculptor Thomas Brock (1847–1922) was incomparably well qualified for the task, and his collaboration with the architect Sir Aston Webb (1849–1930) proved inspired.

The whole composition remains London's grandest set piece of urban planning. The perimeter gates and piers – funded by contributions from Australia,

Canada and South Africa – provided ceremonial entrances to Green Park and St James's Park, ornamented with carved animals and devices peculiar to each realm. The Queen appears enthroned in the marble centrepiece, guarded by eight colossal bronze figures, *Progress* and *Peace*, *Manufacture* and *Agriculture*, *Painting* and *Architecture*, *Shipbuilding* and *War*. These bronzes were still not in place for the unveiling ceremony on 16 May 1911.

By the time the statues were finally installed in 1924, an even more significant addition had been made. Since 1866, the soft Caen stone of Blore's East Wing had been decaying and the sentries often had to shelter in their boxes from falling fragments of masonry. There were many who found the contrast between the gleaming white marble of the Queen Victoria Memorial sculptures and the blackened, flaking façade behind unacceptable. The decision was made to remove the decayed stonework and reface the East Front. In June 1912, Webb and Brock were again instructed to prepare designs. The funds would allow only a refacing and any design would therefore have to respect entirely the proportions of Blore's original front.

In the autumn of 1912, the main contractor, Leslie & Co., began preparing the Portland stone blocks in its yards at Fulham and Vauxhall, while Brock embarked on the carving of the royal arms, which measure 8 metres across, on the central pediment.

The work was planned to coincide with the royal family's absence from London during the summer and early autumn of 1913. When the scaffolding came down, what struck most people was the dramatic transition from black to white; from the sooty darkness of Blore's decayed Caen stone to the hard and reflective surface of the Portland. What had been lost was Blore's picturesque skyline, but Webb's façade was soon regarded as altogether more stately and dignified. The King laid on a supper to thank the 500 workmen who had seen the job to completion and in particular for their having resisted calls to join the strikes that had been threatened during the summer.

As the final component of the memorial scheme, three magnificent pairs of bronze gates were commissioned in 1905 from the Bromsgrove Guild.

With the Queen Victoria Memorial Scheme, the Palace reached its final form. Only a year after the completion of the East Front, the central balcony assumed an unforeseen importance when the King and Queen appeared before massed crowds on 4 August 1914, the day of the outbreak of the First World War.

ABOVE
One of the centre gates under construction in the workshop of the Bromsgrove Guild, c.1905–6.

BELOW
Proposal drawings by Frank Baines (1877–1933) for the remodelling of the Picture Gallery, 1915. The new ceiling design finally resolved the chronic lighting problem and put an end to 25 years of rainwater leaks.

BVCKINGHAM·PALACE
PICTVRE·GALLERY
SCHEME for REDECORATION
VIEW of LOBBY at
SOVTH·EAST·END

During the Second World War, the Palace itself became a target. In April 1940 and repeatedly the following September, bombs fell on parts of the building, destroying the south-western conservatory (Queen Victoria's Private Chapel), together with more than 100 metres of the forecourt railings. These were remade by the Bromsgrove Guild but, in common with much of the rest of London, the buildings themselves could not be repaired for some years. When it became possible to devote resources to the rebuilding of the Chapel, the opportunity was taken to provide a space for public exhibitions from the Royal Collection. The Queen's Gallery, as it became known, was the brainchild of HRH The Duke of Edinburgh and first opened its doors in 1962. Forty years later, after almost five million visitors had enjoyed 38 exhibitions, the Gallery was

redeveloped and considerably enlarged to a new design by John Simpson (b.1954) to celebrate The Queen's Golden Jubilee.

The Occupants of Buckingham Palace

QUEEN VICTORIA (1837–1901) AND PRINCE ALBERT (1840–1861)

RIGHT Louis Haghe (1806–85), *The 1745 Fancy Ball at Buckingham Palace, 6 June 1845.* Watercolour. The Queen (in a blue sash) and Prince Albert (in a blue sash and red coat) dance the royal minuet in the Throne Room.

Queen Victoria succeeded her uncle, William IV, on 20 June 1837, at the age of only 18. On 13 July, she left Kensington Palace, her childhood home, and became the first Sovereign to rule from Buckingham Palace. Although the Palace was habitable, the private apartments were far from complete and remained so until after the Queen's marriage in 1840 to her cousin, Prince Albert of Saxe-Coburg and Gotha.

The young Queen was determined to make use of the newly completed, colourful state rooms and the regular balls at the Palace became a centrepiece of the London season. In the first decades of her reign, the Queen was an enthusiastic dancer, often staying up until the small hours of the morning. Grand and spectacular as all the occasions were, the conditions in the Throne Room, Picture Gallery and Blue Drawing Room were cramped, and the numerous candles gave off both heat and liberal quantities of wax, which stuck to the wigs and heavy gowns of the guests. During

OPPOSITE
Franz Xaver Winterhalter (1805–73), *The Royal Family in 1846.* Queen Victoria, Prince Albert and their five eldest children.

RIGHT
Louis Haghe, *The Picture Gallery in Use for a Banquet in Honour of the Christening of Prince Leopold in 1853*, 1858. Watercolour.

her travels in Europe, Queen Victoria had taken note of the condition and capacity of the continental palaces. This inspired the construction of the new Ballroom, which was added to the south side of the Palace in 1855.

Over the course of 20 years, Queen Victoria and Prince Albert transformed what they had taken on as a previously uninhabited and architecturally incomplete palace into the centre of an energetic, cosmopolitan court. The unceasing round of ceremonial and state occasions went hand in hand with the complete internal redecoration of the Palace in an advanced Renaissance revival style, and the introduction of new technology. In 1856, the future Prime Minister, Benjamin Disraeli (1804–81), declared upon first seeing Pennethorne's new Ballroom in action, 'I had never seen before in England anything which realised my idea of a splendid court.'

Although the series of state concerts continued in the Ballroom after Prince Albert's death, all other entertainments ceased. As the Queen spent lengthy periods at Windsor, Osborne or Balmoral, the Palace fell into a long period of inactivity. The brightly coloured interiors gradually darkened as the century, and the reign, drew to a close.

LEFT
Prince Albert, Queen Victoria and Charles, Prince of Leiningen (1804–56; the Queen's half-brother) in costumes of the period of Charles II for the ball of 1851. This is Queen Victoria's own watercolour sketch from her Journal.

MUSIC AT COURT

BELOW
Programme for a concert in the Ballroom, 1858. The concerts were given by Queen Victoria's private band of 24 players, supplemented by musicians from the leading London orchestras.

Originally named the 'Ball and Concert Room', the Ballroom was also intended for large-scale musical performances. Both the Queen and Prince Albert were competent and devoted musicians and more than 100 orchestral concerts were given at the Palace in the course of Queen Victoria's reign.

During a state ball, two or three orchestras would be disposed around the state apartments. In 1838, the Austrian composer and conductor, Johann Strauss the Elder (1804–89), composed his Tribute to Queen Victoria of Great Britain, including a waltz-time version of the national anthem. In the previous year, the 25-year-old Sigismund Thalberg (1812–71) – 'the most famous pianist in the world', as the Queen described him in her Journal – had her 'quite in ecstasies and raptures' as she listened to his playing.

Felix Mendelssohn (1809–47) visited on five occasions between 1842 and 1847, each time playing for the royal couple and sometimes listening to or accompanying their own singing.

ABOVE
Late nineteenth-century photograph of the Ballroom prepared for a state concert.

LEFT
Ernst Rietschel (1804–61), *Felix Mendelssohn*, c.1848. Marble.

KING EDWARD VII AND QUEEN ALEXANDRA (1901–1910)

Long in waiting as Prince of Wales, the new King Edward VII moved into Buckingham Palace shortly after his mother's death in January 1901, with an impact that was later described as like that of a Viennese hussar bursting suddenly into an English vicarage. Declaring with a characteristic roll of his 'r's, 'I don't know much about *arrt*, but I think I know something about *arr*angement', he set about the complete redecoration of the interior in a universal white-and-gold finish. The Surveyor of The King's Works of Art, Sir Lionel Henry Cust (1859–1929), meanwhile saw to the overhaul of the furnishings, and improvements were put in hand to the heating, ventilation and electric lighting. By March 1902, court life was resumed. There were some reforms, such as the King's abolition of afternoon Drawing Rooms in favour of Evening Courts, which suited his routine far better and allowed more grandeur of costume, even if still within the strict rules laid down by the Lord Chamberlain. It was decided that the 60-year-old King should preside at Evening Courts seated on the throne and a new dais and canopy were set up in the Ballroom for this purpose. The long series of state concerts that had taken place in the Ballroom since its completion in 1856 now came to an end. King Edward had become accustomed to the more cosmopolitan allure of the dance bands employed by his friends such as Alfred de Rothschild. He abolished the King's Private Band and invited outside ensembles to perform during Evening Courts and at balls.

LEFT

Sir Samuel Luke Fildes (1843–1927), *King Edward VII*, 1902.

ABOVE
Sketch by Sir John Lavery
(1856–1941) for his large
group portrait, *The Royal
Family at Buckingham
Palace*, 1913, set in the
White Drawing Room.

For Queen Mary (1867–1953), Buckingham Palace, which she had left on the day of her marriage to the Duke of York in 1893, was a place of fond memories, but the move from Marlborough House, which she and her husband had occupied during the reign of King Edward VII, was no less daunting. She wrote soon after moving in to the Palace, 'Everything here is so straggly, such distances and so fatiguing' and recalled later that 'many things were changed here much too quickly by our predecessors … it is always best to do such things very *piano* and with much reflection'. Nevertheless, at Buckingham Palace Queen Mary was able to indulge her 'one great hobby', researching and organising the Royal Collection.

During the early years of King George V's reign (1910–36), the Palace was often the backdrop against which great issues were played out. In July 1914, the King convened a conference in an attempt to bring together the parties involved in deciding on the boundaries of what became the province of Northern Ireland. In May of that year, the long-running campaign for Women's Suffrage was given greater prominence by the arrest of its leader, Emmeline Pankhurst, outside the Palace gates as she sought to deliver a petition to the King.

In 1935, the King celebrated his Silver Jubilee with an exultant nation. Commemorative events and initiatives were held throughout the country, for which the Palace once again provided a focus.

ABOVE
Queen Mary inspects
a parade of women
landworkers in the
Quadrangle, March 1918.

LEFT
Mrs Emmeline Pankhurst
is arrested as she
attempts to deliver a
petition on women's
suffrage to King George V,
May 1914.

KING GEORGE VI AND QUEEN ELIZABETH (1936–1952)

The reign of King George VI (1936–52) was dominated by the Second World War, for the duration of which the normal life of the Palace was suspended. The King and Queen's decision to remain in residence during the intense bombing of London in 1940 was an inspiration to the country. In the early months of 1940, Queen Elizabeth (1900–2002) gave several sittings to the painter Augustus John (1878–1961) in the Yellow Drawing Room on the East Front, but these were suspended because – as the Queen's Private Secretary noted – the temperature in the room was 'indistinguishable to that reported in Finland'.

During Germany's night offensive on London, from early September to mid-November 1940, when London was attacked by an average of 160 bombers per night, the King and Queen left the Palace each evening for Windsor, returning in the morning. Together they ventured out to visit bomb-damaged communities in east and south London, encouraging those who had lost their homes in the task of rebuilding.

When the European war finally ended on 8 May 1945, the King and Queen and the Princesses Elizabeth and Margaret Rose appeared on the balcony before unprecedented crowds, returning eight times during the day and evening, a scene that was repeated when hostilities finally came to an end in the Far East, on 15 August, VJ Day. As the former routine of the Palace began to recover, the King broadcast his Christmas message in reassuring terms: 'This Christmas is a real homecoming to us all, a return to a world in which the homely and friendly things of life are again to be ours.'

HER MAJESTY THE QUEEN AND HRH THE DUKE OF EDINBURGH (FROM 1952)

After their marriage in November 1947, The Princess Elizabeth and The Duke of Edinburgh lived temporarily at Buckingham Palace while Clarence House was refurbished, following its wartime use by the British Red Cross and Order of St John. In November 1948, The Prince of Wales was born at the Palace, moving with his parents to Clarence House in 1949. The sudden death of the King in February 1952 brought the new Queen and her husband to

occupy Buckingham Palace on a permanent basis, which they have now done for far longer than any other royal couple.

The decisively forward-looking mood of the early years of The Queen's reign, in the wake of the Festival of Britain of 1951 and the rapid pace of social change, was mirrored in the simplification of many aspects of court life. In 1958, the practice of presentation at court, at which debutantes were presented to

LEFT
Trooping the Colour outside the Palace to mark The Queen's Official Birthday in June.

29

THE OCCUPANTS OF BUCKINGHAM PALACE

RIGHT
The Queen's Coronation procession, 2 June 1953.

LEFT
The Queen and The Duke of Edinburgh with the President of the United States and Mrs Obama during the State Visit in May 2011. The Queen, as Head of State, receives a large number of formal and informal visits during the year, from the Privy Council, foreign and British ambassadors and high commissioners, members of the clergy, and senior officers of the armed services and the civil service.

The Queen at receptions in the state rooms, was discontinued. This decision was taken not because such ceremonies were outdated, but rather because the overwhelming number of applications meant that some form of selection – which would have been invidious – would have had to be applied.

The present reign has been characterised by the extent to which The Queen and The Duke of Edinburgh have travelled, including more than 80 state visits, 160 overseas visits and innumerable journeys around the United Kingdom. Meanwhile, well over a million people have attended the annual garden parties.

Essential works of modernisation have been accompanied by subtle decorative changes within the Palace. The fireplaces were converted to electricity in 1956 and the Picture Gallery, Silk Tapestry Room and State Dining Room were redecorated. In 1962, The Queen's Gallery was created from the ruins of the former Private Chapel. The Gallery provides members of the public with opportunities to see works of art from Buckingham Palace as well as Windsor,

OPPOSITE
Her Majesty The Queen and HRH Duke of Edinburgh in the White Drawing Room, 1966. Photograph by Yousuf Karsh (1908–2002).

Holyroodhouse and the unoccupied royal palaces. In 1993, The Queen decided that the Palace itself should be opened for the summer months in order to raise funds for the great task of reconstructing Windsor Castle following the disastrous fire the previous November. Since the completion of the restoration in 1997, revenues from the annual Summer Opening have been directed to the care and maintenance of the Royal Collection and to major capital projects, chief among them the rebuilding of The Queen's Gallery and its counterpart in Edinburgh.

LEFT
The Palace lit up for the Golden Jubilee, 2002.

Tour of the Palace

EAST FRONT, AMBASSADORS' COURT AND QUADRANGLE

RIGHT
Changing of the Guard on the forecourt.

OPPOSITE
The internal façade of Edward Blore's East Wing. The central pediment incorporates sculptures that originally faced the Mall as part of Nash's design. The façade was restored in 2009–10 to reveal the original Caen stone.

The East Front of the Palace remains exactly as it was after the refacing operation of 1913. The central arch is reserved for use by the Sovereign on the most important ceremonial occasions, while the two lower arches and their pedestrian side arches are in regular use. At the extreme right-hand (northern) end of the main façade is the Privy Purse Door, where those on official business with the Royal Household are admitted. The Side Door, located on the south side of the Palace, receives all deliveries and trade vehicles.

PRESENTATION AT COURT

Since the Middle Ages, access to the person of the Sovereign has been controlled by the senior official of the Royal Household, the Lord Chamberlain. The system of regular assemblies of those seeking the Lord Chamberlain's leave to be presented to the monarch dates from the reign of Queen Anne (1702–14), when afternoon Drawing Rooms were instituted at St James's Palace. These continued throughout the eighteenth and nineteenth centuries, in parallel with regular morning Levées, which took place twice weekly and were for men only. King Edward VII replaced the Drawing Rooms with Evening Courts, which remained a central part of the London social season until 1939. Dress regulations were very strictly adhered to and these occasions provided widespread employment among dressmakers and official tailors. Presentation at court was resumed in 1947 in the form of a Presentation Garden Party, which from 1949 was held in the state apartments. During this period, the parties were specifically designed for debutantes in their first London season. In 1958, Presentation Parties were discontinued and replaced by additional garden parties.

LEFT
Foreign diplomats and their ladies arriving at the Ambassadors' Entrance for a Drawing Room, *Illustrated London News*, August 1868.

THE CHANGING OF THE GUARD

This ceremony, in which the soldiers who have been on duty at St James's Palace and Buckingham Palace (the Old Guard) are relieved by the New Guard, takes place at 11.00am on the forecourt. In autumn and winter, the ceremony is held on alternate days.

The Queen's Guard is made up from the five regiments of Foot Guards: the Grenadier, Coldstream, Scots, Irish and Welsh Guards. The ceremony has the following stages:

11.00 Both detachments of the Old Guard parade and are inspected at Buckingham Palace and St James's.

11.15 The St James's Palace detachment of the Old Guard marches to Buckingham Palace with a band.

11.30 The New Guard arrives at Buckingham Palace from Wellington Barracks led by a band. During the transfer of duties, the band plays a selection of music.

12.05 The Old Guard leaves Buckingham Palace for Wellington Barracks accompanied by the band.

BELOW
E.H. Shepard (1879–1976), *Christopher Robin Saluting Guardsman.*

LEFT
Ambassadors' Court.

The visitor enters the Palace via the Ambassadors' Entrance, which was designed by Edward Blore. As its name suggests, this entrance was reserved for foreign ambassadors to the court of St James's and others with the special privilege known as the entrée, such as senior members of the Government and of the diplomatic or armed services.

Before the addition of Queen Victoria's new wing, the Quadrangle was open on the side facing the Mall, with the Marble Arch at the centre. The wings to the north and south are part of Nash's original building. The north wing is devoted to the offices of the Lord Chamberlain and Private Secretary's departments, with domestic accommodation above. The south wing contains the offices of the Master of the Household and Privy Purse departments, with further accommodation on the chamber storey. It is in the Quadrangle that carriage processions form up on ceremonial occasions such as the State Opening of Parliament. During a state visit, the mounted band of the Household Division plays here to welcome the carriages containing the visitor and their suite.

LEFT
The Queen's carriage procession forming in the Quadrangle for the State Opening of Parliament.

THE ROYAL COLLECTION

The entire contents of the Palace – from the chairs and desks used in many of the offices to the most outstanding paintings and works of art displayed in the state rooms – form part of the Royal Collection, which is held by The Queen as Sovereign for her successors and the nation. Shaped by the personal tastes of kings and queens over more than five centuries, it remains a working collection unlike any other. The Royal Collection provides the backdrop for official and ceremonial events and offers the public a rare opportunity to enjoy works of art in the historic settings for which they were intended. In addition, special exhibitions are presented at The Queen's Galleries in London and Edinburgh, while over 3,000 objects from the Royal Collection are on short- and long-term loan to museums and galleries around the United Kingdom and abroad. The Collection Online (www.royalcollection.org.uk/art) offers on-demand details of thousands of works in the Collection.

The revenues from the public opening of the Palace are received by the Royal Collection Trust, whose chief aims are to preserve and conserve the Collection and to make it as widely available as possible.

RIGHT
The exhibition
*Victoria and Albert:
Art and Love* at The
Queen's Gallery,
London, 2010.

BELOW
Prince William and his bride Catherine Middleton arrive under the *porte-cochère* at Buckingham Palace after their wedding at Westminster Abbey, 29 April 2011, before entering the state rooms for the official photographs.

The term 'state rooms' is applied to those rooms that were designed and built as the public rooms of the Palace, in which the Sovereign receives, rewards and entertains her subjects and visiting dignitaries. The state rooms occupy the heart of the Palace and most of what lies beyond them is devoted to subsidiary, service functions.

A second, complementary purpose of the state rooms is for the display of some of the most outstanding works of art in the Royal Collection, which provide a permanent and magnificent backdrop to the events that take place here. This has always been the primary function of the Collection and, as well as allowing for the display of pictures and furniture throughout the apartments, Nash included two purpose-built galleries, for paintings and sculpture, at the very heart of the Palace, one above the other.

GRAND ENTRANCE AND GRAND HALL

ABOVE
Detail of one of the state room doors. Nash's exuberant design for the doors, ornamented with the motif of a crown in a sunburst, appears throughout the state rooms and was perpetuated by Pennethorne for his new rooms of the 1850s, when the varied use of plain or mirrored glass was exploited so as to create apparently infinite vistas.

The principal entry to the Palace via the *porte-cochère* or covered carriage entrance, the Grand Entrance forms the lower half of the two-storey portico designed by Nash at the centre of the building. It is here that ambassadors drive in carriages several times a week for audiences with The Queen on taking up or relinquishing their posts in London. The Queen's guests arrive by this entrance for garden parties or evening receptions, and it is also in the Grand Hall that The Queen welcomes heads of state and presents the senior members of her Household on the first day of a state visit. On these occasions the scene is enlivened by superb floral arrangements; the scarlet cloaks, gold livery and top hats of the footmen and state porters; and the burnished steel breastplates and plumed helmets of The Queen's Bodyguard.

The decoration of this room and the other main circulation spaces conforms to the white, red and gold scheme introduced by King Edward VII soon after his accession

in 1901. The marble statues were also introduced by King Edward VII, who had them brought from Osborne, his parents' house on the Isle of Wight, after it had been presented to the nation in 1902. All four of the statues were commissioned by Queen Victoria or Prince Albert from artists working in Rome.

ABOVE
At a cost of £1,000, the most expensive single element of the Grand Hall was the chimneypiece, carved by Joseph Theakston (1772–1842).

'MARBLED HALLS'

In total, 104 columns were deployed in the Grand Hall and in the adjoining Marble Hall. Each was formed of a single block of marble quarried in Tuscany under the supervision of the mason Joseph Browne. The *Evening Standard* of 26 September 1829 reported the arrival of one particularly large block, weighing 24 tonnes, which was hauled to the Palace from the wharf at Millbank by a team of 17 horses.

ABOVE
Eugène Lami (1800–90), *The Grand Staircase at Buckingham Palace, State Ball, 5 July 1848.* Watercolour. In 1846, Prince Albert instituted a new polychrome scheme, which can be seen clearly in Eugène Lami's splendid view of the arrivals at the Ball, but this in its turn was effaced by King Edward VII's campaign of 1902.

When compared with those of the many aristocratic town houses built in London at around the same time, the staircase at Buckingham Palace occupies a notably confined space. This allowed Nash to place more emphasis on the vertical dimension and to draw on his experience of London theatres, where space in front of the auditorium was usually at a premium. The transition from the comparative darkness of the Grand Hall to the bright daylight of the staircase imparts a sense of excitement and expectation. The stairs are lit by a shallow dome of glass etched with figures of angels.

Queen Victoria fitted into the walls around the upper part of the stairs the series of full-length portraits of members of her immediate family, including her grandparents, George III and Queen Charlotte, her parents, the Duke (1767–1820) and Duchess of Kent (1786–1861), and her predecessor on the throne, her uncle William IV, and his wife Queen Adelaide (1792–1849). The portraits serve almost as a perpetual 'receiving line', so that whoever climbs the staircase is introduced to Queen Victoria's family.

BELOW
Emil Wolff (1802–79),
Prince Albert, 1846.
Marble. This is the
second version of a
sculpture given by Prince
Albert to Queen Victoria
for her birthday in 1842.
In the original, the Prince
wears a shorter kilt,
and no sandals – the
modification in this
version was due to
the Prince's sense
that the statue was
'too undressed'.

At the top of the stairs, the first of many pairs of glazed mahogany doors leads to a room known as the Guard Chamber.

In baroque palaces of the late seventeenth century, such as Hampton Court or Charles II's Windsor, a guard chamber was invariably to be found at the top of the stairs, providing a secure barrier to the following rooms, which allowed increasing degrees of access to the royal presence. Although Nash laid out the state rooms here on this basic pattern, such formalities were already a thing of the past. In any case, had George IV survived to use his new Palace, no great company of guards could have been accommodated in this small room, which is one of the most exquisitely wrought of all Nash's interiors. With its ceiling consisting of 28 fitted, curved and deeply cut glass lights set into a matrix of gilded plaster ornaments, it resembles the inside of a giant jewel casket. The two marble statues of Queen Victoria and Prince Albert were installed here in 1849.

ABOVE
The Guard Chamber is more symbolic than useful but, with its apsed ends, Carrara marble columns and richly decorated plaster ceiling, it forms an architectural overture to the glories to come.

GREEN DRAWING ROOM

ABOVE
Francis Cotes (1726–70),
*Princess Louisa Ann and
Princess Caroline Matilda*
(sisters of George III),
1767.

In the Green Drawing Room, Nash divided the walls with entirely abstract pilasters of lattice plasterwork, gilded and filled with thousands of separately cast and applied florets. Nash's pilasters support an equally abstracted frieze of garlands and swags, beneath a robustly geometric ceiling. To the critic Allan Cunningham, writing in *Fraser's Magazine* in 1830, the ceilings of the new Palace (which were not all completed by then) were 'in a style new in this country, partaking very much of the boldest style in the Italian taste of the fifteenth century … It is indeed not easy to conceive anything more splendid.' All of the applied plasterwork was supplied by the London firm of George Jackson & Sons, while William Croggon inlaid the borders around the edge of the floor in holly and satinwood.

The only features of the room that post-date Nash's original conception are the tall carved and gilt overmantel mirrors, which probably date from the 1830s. The room has always been hung with green silk. Originally this was of the quality known as 'tabinet', woven in Ireland in 1834 on the special instruction of Queen Adelaide, wife of William IV. This was replaced in 1864, together with the green and gold silk curtains and valances. Further replacements have followed roughly every 30 years since, with some variation in the pattern. One of the decorative innovations of the Prince Regent's Carlton House interiors has been perpetuated here, with groups of green-ground Sèvres porcelain vases deployed to match the wall coverings, while blue-ground vases may be found in the Blue Drawing Room.

ABOVE
Sèvres soft-paste porcelain pot-pourri vase in the form of a ship, 1758. One of the rarest and most distinctive pieces of Sèvres porcelain in the Royal Collection, it originally belonged to Madame de Pompadour (1721–64), Louis XV's mistress, and was subsequently acquired by George IV in Paris in 1817 for 2,500 francs.

RIGHT
Adam Weisweiler (1744–1820), Cabinet with *pietra dura* panels, *c*.1780–85. Enriched with seventeenth-century panels of *pietra dura* (hardstone), the cabinet was probably bought by George IV for Carlton House in 1791. Some of the panels, such as the two with single flowers, may have been made in Florence, while those in relief may have come from the Gobelins manufactory in Paris.

THRONE ROOM

Of all Nash's interiors at Buckingham Palace, this is one of the most dramatic and convincing. Everything seems contrived to focus the eye on the throne dais and canopy, in effect a stage for the pageantry of monarchy. The canopy and thrones are separated from the body of the room by a proscenium arch, from which two life-size winged *genii* hold the garlanded initials of George IV.

The medieval character of the friezes and heraldry recalls the richly historical pageantry of George IV's coronation in 1821, when the King and his court processed to Westminster Abbey in extravagant medieval costumes. Here in the Throne Room at Buckingham Palace, the most theatrical monarch in

British history was ably served by the genius of theatre architecture, John Nash. The plaster bust of his younger brother, who succeeded him as William IV in 1830, occupies the place of honour in the doorcase opposite the throne. Queen Victoria was the first monarch to make use of the Throne Room; with its chandeliers lit by over 200 candles, it was the central setting for the spectacular costume balls of the 1840s. Later, in the reign of King George V, the Throne Room was used for investitures. The modern crimson silk hangings represent a return to the original scheme for the room; for much of the last century the walls were painted a light stone colour.

PICTURE GALLERY

The four marble chimneypieces each support a garlanded medallion of one of the great painters: Titian and Leonardo da Vinci at the northern end of the gallery, and Dürer and Van Dyck at the southern end.

By placing this great gallery at the very centre of the Palace, Nash created a worthy and prominent setting for George IV's picture collection. Despite the outstanding quality of the pictures – by Holbein, Rembrandt, Rubens, Canaletto and others – this has never been a gallery in which the works of art are intended to be regarded with the sort of hushed reverence that reigns in museums. Nash planned it on the first floor so that it could act as one of the principal reception rooms of the Palace, a role it still performs today, for several hundred guests at a time. The gallery is also occasionally used for banquets in support of charities or organisations with royal patrons, and throughout the year it is here that the recipients of honours assemble before being led into the Ballroom for investitures.

A second important reason for the location of the gallery was to take advantage of natural light from above ('top-lighting'), which by the early nineteenth century was considered essential for the viewing of pictures. The gallery was declared ready for hanging with pictures by Christmas 1835.

By the end of the nineteenth century, Blore's central glazing had begun to let in rainwater, but it was not until 1914–15 that it was replaced by the present design.

Several colour schemes have been employed in the Picture Gallery. Early views show a warm biscuit colour, which was also used at that time on the Grand Staircase. Under Prince Albert's direction, the walls were painted in lilac in 1851 and the ceiling picked out in terracotta and blue. King Edward VII hung the gallery with bright yellow silk, which King George V replaced in green following the remodelling of 1915. When these hangings had become faded by 1946, the decision was taken simply to rehang them back to front, an instance of post-war economy. The present decorative scheme dates from 1964.

The Picture Gallery in 1910. The circular rooflights to the sides survive from Nash's design. The central square lights were introduced by Blore.

A ROYAL COLLECTOR

The 47-metre gallery now contains works from many periods, almost all of them acquired by one of the four most important royal collectors of pictures: George IV; his father George III and grandfather Frederick, Prince of Wales (1707–51); and the greatest of them all, Charles I. Charles I's collection was auctioned by the Parliamentary authorities after his execution in 1649, and although two Van Dyck portraits and many others were subsequently returned to the Royal Collection, the majority of his pictures remain dispersed in other collections throughout Europe and North America.

Sir Peter Paul Rubens (1577–1640), *Self-portrait*, 1623. This self-portrait was sent by Rubens to Charles I.

PAINTINGS FROM THE ROYAL COLLECTION

OPPOSITE
Johannes Vermeer (1632–75), *A Lady at the Virginals with a Gentleman ('The Music Lesson')*, c.1662–5.

BELOW LEFT
Jan Steen (1626–79), *A Woman at her Toilet*, 1663.

LEFT
Sir Peter Paul Rubens (1577–1640), *Milkmaid with Cattle in a Landscape: 'The Farm at Laken'*, 1617–18.

BELOW RIGHT
Rembrandt van Rijn (1606–69), *Agatha Bas*, 1640.

RIGHT
Lorenzo Lotto (*c.*1480–1556), *Andrea Odoni*, 1527.

FAR RIGHT
Antonio Canaletto, (1697–1768), *The Piazzetta towards the Torre dell'Orologico*, *c.*1728.

RIGHT
Rembrandt van Rijn (1606–69), *Portrait of Jan Rijcksen and his Wife, Griet Jans ('The Shipbuilder and his Wife')*, 1633.

OPPOSITE
Aelbert Cuyp (1620–91), *The Passage Boat*, *c.*1650

SILK TAPESTRY ROOM

The Silk Tapestry Room serves to connect Nash's state apartments with the rooms added for Queen Victoria in 1856. The single seventeenth-century Italian embroidery panel in the Picture Gallery Lobby formerly hung, with three others, in this room, and although these were moved elsewhere in 1965 when the room was redecorated, the old name has been retained.

DOROTHY JORDAN

Dorothy (Dora) Jordan (1761–1816) was the greatest comic actress of her generation and the mistress of William, Duke of Clarence, by whom she had five sons and five daughters. They took the name Fitzclarence and the eldest son, George Augustus Frederick (1794–1842), was created Earl of Munster in 1831. The Duke of Clarence dismissed Dora in 1812 and she died in penury in France four years later. One of the Duke's first acts on succeeding as William IV in 1830 was to summon Sir Francis Chantrey to create a marble monument to Mrs Jordan in which the quality of 'maternal affection' should be emphasised. It was intended to stand in Westminster Abbey, but this was not allowed and the statue passed down in Dora's family until 1975, when it was bequeathed to The Queen by the 5th Earl of Munster. It was placed at the end of the Picture Gallery in 1980.

LEFT
Sir Francis Chantrey (1781–1841), *Mrs Jordan and Two of her Children*, 1834. Marble.

EAST GALLERY

On leaving the Silk Tapestry Room, the visitor enters the principal Victorian addition to the Palace, which was built on and around the site of the libraries that George III's architect, Sir William Chambers (1723–96), added to Buckingham House at the end of the eighteenth century. Once George III's books had been presented to the nation by his son George IV, these fine rooms became redundant.

Sir James Pennethorne's design for the East or 'Promenade' Gallery drew on the architectural vocabulary developed for the Palace by his former employer John Nash. As well as replicating Nash's glazed mahogany doors and the use of top-lighting, Pennethorne made use of a fifth marble chimneypiece of the same design as those in the Picture Gallery, this time with a medallion of Rembrandt. The gallery is now hung with a selection of paintings of previous monarchs, from Charles I onwards.

BELOW
Sir George Hayter (1792–1871), *The Coronation of Queen Victoria, 28 June 1838*, 1839.

BALL SUPPER ROOM

Once it had been decided to build a new Ballroom for Queen Victoria, the provision of a Supper Room on a scale sufficient to provide refreshment for several hundred guests at a time was necessary. The design of both rooms was undertaken by Pennethorne and it was the Supper Room that finally put paid to the shell of George III's Octagon Library, which formerly occupied this site. Pennethorne's design envisaged a continuous serving table 41 metres in length arranged in a horseshoe shape.

Today, the Ball Supper Room is used as a ballroom during The Queen's Diplomatic Reception and Christmas Dance. When the Palace is open during August and September, a special display is mounted here as part of the tour of the state rooms.

BALLROOM

OPPOSITE

The Ballroom set up for a state banquet.

When first completed in 1855, this enormous room, measuring 14 metres high, 34 long and 18 wide was known as the Ball and Concert Room. It was first used for a ball on 8 May 1856. The musicians' gallery is today occupied during investitures by musicians of the Household Division.

At the other end of the room, plaster statues by William Theed (1804–91) stand on top of a triumphal arch, flanked by sphinxes and enclosing the throne canopy. The winged figures at the summit of the arch symbolise History and Fame. They support a medallion with the profiles of Queen Victoria and Prince Albert. The throne canopy was created in 1916 using heavy gold embroidered velvet hangings salvaged from the imperial canopy, or *shamiana*, made for King George V and Queen Mary's appearance at the Delhi Durbar of 1911. The present hangings were supplied by the London firm of Heal & Sons in 1967. When the Ballroom was originally completed, gas-lit pendants by Osler of Birmingham were fitted in the ceiling panels, while further gas appliances were placed behind the windows at the upper level. The present chandeliers were supplied in 1907.

The painted decoration of the organ case is all that survives of the elaborate scheme devised for the room by Prince Albert with

THE ORGAN

Originally supplied in 1817 for the Music Room at Brighton Pavilion, the organ was moved here after Queen Victoria sold the Pavilion in 1848. The organ was rebuilt and extended by Gray & Davison and installed in a case designed by Pennethorne, flanked by plaster figures symbolising Music and modelled by Theed. The gilt plaster roundels represent George Frederick Handel (1685–1759), whose music had been championed at the English court ever since the reign of George III. The latest restoration of the organ was completed in time for The Queen's Golden Jubilee in 2002 and it has subsequently been used for broadcasts and performances.

his artistic adviser Ludwig Gruner.

Each year the Ballroom is the setting for 20 investiture ceremonies, at which the recipients of honours published in The Queen's New Year and Birthday Honours Lists are invested with their insignia by The Queen, for whom The Prince of Wales sometimes deputises.

On the evening of the first day of a state visit, The Queen entertains the visiting head of state at a banquet in the Ballroom, at which 160 guests are seated at a long U-shaped table. These full dress occasions are part of a tradition of royal hospitality that is as old as the institution of monarchy itself. The tables are ornamented with the finest silver-gilt plate from the Royal Collection and a magnificent 'buffet' of embossed dishes, cups and sconces is set up on long sideboards to either side of the room.

There are two entrances to the Ballroom, recalling the architecture of a medieval Great Hall: the door from the East Gallery leads to the 'lower' end of the Ballroom and is the general entrance, while the door from the Throne end leads through the rooms along the West Front to the private

The insignia of the Order of the British Empire:

ABOVE LEFT
The Gentlemen's insignia.

ABOVE RIGHT
The Ladies' insignia.

BELOW
Louis Haghe, *The New Ballroom at Buckingham Palace*, 1856. Watercolour.

apartments. At investiture ceremonies, The Queen and her attendants enter via the West Gallery to stand on the dais, but at state banquets The Queen leads her principal guest and others in a procession from the main body of the state apartments into the Ballroom via the East Gallery.

The West Gallery was designed by Pennethorne as a link with Nash's state rooms, whose style it follows closely.

THE QUEEN AS 'FOUNT OF HONOUR'

The award of honours recognises service to the nation and community by individuals or groups in all walks of society. The Order of the Garter (founded 1348), Order of the Thistle (revived 1687), Order of Merit (founded 1902), Royal Victorian Order (founded 1896) and Royal Victorian Chain are in The Queen's personal gift. Other honours, including appointments to the Orders of the Bath (1725), St Michael and St George (1818), and the Order of the British Empire (1917), are made on the advice of ministers.

Within the British honours system, to be knighted or appointed a dame allows a gentleman to bear the title 'Sir' and a lady the title 'Dame'. Most honours and decorations also allow the bearer to place letters after their name, such as OBE.

STATE DINING ROOM

The great advantage of the rooms on the west side of the Palace is the view of the garden. Late on a summer afternoon, the rooms are flooded with sunlight and filled with fresh air, often carrying the scent of new-mown grass and instilling a unique sense of *rus in urbe*, the phrase that was carved on the cornice of the Duke of Buckingham's house on this site.

The initials of both William IV and Queen Victoria appearing in roundels in the cove are indications that this room was among the last to be completed after the death of George IV in 1830 brought the construction of the Palace to an abrupt but temporary halt.

The design of the ceiling is by Blore. The ornaments, some of which were made in gilded papier mâché, are generally looser and more florid than Nash's. Blore also designed the overdoors and the matching picture frames containing a series of paired portraits of the Hanoverian sovereigns and consorts from George I to George IV. Space, and perhaps discretion, prevented the inclusion of George IV's 'unruly queen', Caroline of Brunswick (1768–1821). As on the Grand Staircase, this arrangement was Queen Victoria's idea.

Before the creation of the Ballroom, the deep recess at the southern end of the State Dining Room housed the buffet on which a display of gold plate would be mounted for important dinners. Since Queen Victoria's reign the room has been used for dining on special occasions.

LEFT
Douglas Morison, *The State Dining Room*, 1847 (detail). The walls of the State Dining Room were originally painted a warm stone colour, which was first replaced with crimson damask in 1965–6.

RIGHT
William Pitts (1790–1840),
Plaster group celebrating
William Shakespeare,
c.1835.

Nash's plan provided two large drawing rooms, known simply as the North and South Drawing Rooms, either side of the central Bay Drawing Room. These rooms are now known respectively as the White and Blue Drawing Rooms and the Music Room. The Blue Drawing Room was effectively the ballroom of the Palace before Pennethorne's additions of 1855–6. The room must originally have been even more startling. The 30 columns were made by Joseph Browne in scagliola of a colour variously described as 'porphyry' and 'raspberry', the walls were hung with crimson silk and the

A CELEBRATION OF POETRY

The plaster sculpture that is such a feature of the interior of the Palace reaches new heights in the four large arched spaces above the cornice containing figures by Pitts. William Shakespeare, John Milton and Edmund Spenser are each enthroned in triumph, accompanied by nymphs and cherubs. The fourth relief is a generalised evocation of the art of poetry. It is remarkable that the principal drawing room of the British Sovereign celebrated the nation's poets rather than its military might.

curtains and pelmets were of crimson velvet. The columns were painted in 1860 to resemble onyx, in itself a masterpiece of *trompe-l'oeil*, while the blue flock wallpaper was hung at the direction of Queen Mary. The marble chimneypiece with boldly carved foliage and classical motifs is attributed to Sir Richard Westmacott (1775–1856).

FAR LEFT
The Table of The Grand Commanders (1806–12). Made from hard-paste Sèvres porcelain with gilt-bronze mounts, the table top is decorated with portraits of Alexander the Great and 12 other great commanders of antiquity, painted by Louis-Bertin Parant (active 1806–41). The table was commissioned by Napoleon in 1806, when he was the conqueror of all Europe and recently crowned emperor, but it was not finished until 1812 and remained in the Sèvres factory until after Napoleon's final defeat in 1815. Two years later it was presented to George IV by Louis XVIII (1755–1824), in gratitude for the allied victory over Napoleon.

MUSIC ROOM

The Music Room lies at the centre of the West Front, facing the garden. Ranged around its walls are 16 scagliola columns, imitating lapis lazuli. The frieze here and in the two adjoining drawing rooms incorporates a device formed of a triangle within a garland, which is entirely original and may derive from masonic imagery. Both Nash and his patron George IV were Freemasons.

Above the frieze are three more plaster reliefs of infants by William Pitts, representing the Progress of Rhetoric. The subjects are *Eloquence*, *Pleasure* and *Harmony*.

The Music Room is used occasionally for private recitals and plays a more general part in royal entertaining in conjunction with the other state apartments. The modern grand piano is by John Broadwood & Sons. The room is also used for royal christenings. The Queen's three eldest children and her grandson Prince William were baptised here by the Archbishop of Canterbury with water brought from the River Jordan.

The Music Room floor is an outstanding example of parquetry by Thomas Seddon, later of the firm of Morel & Seddon. Inlaid with holly, rosewood, tulipwood and satinwood, it cost £2,187 3s. In his evidence to the Parliamentary Select Committee on the Buckingham Palace project in 1831, Seddon proudly predicted that 'at fifty years hence it would be as good as it is now; you might drive carriages over it'. Featuring the cipher of George IV (above left), it is a triumph of English craftsmanship and one of the finest of its type in Britain.

RIGHT
Sèvres porcelain *vase à batons rompus*, 1764, acquired by George IV. The painted scene is copied from the work of the Dutch seventeenth-century artist David Teniers the Younger (1610–90).

BELOW

Detail of the *pietra dura* plaques on one of the four pier cabinets found on the end walls.

by Adam Weisweiler, and incorporate panels of *pietra dura*. They were extended for use here by the addition of the side shelves and one of them (in the north-western corner) was incorporated into a concealed door. When opened, the mirror and cabinet move as one to provide members of the Royal Family with a discreet means of entering the state rooms from the private rooms beyond. It is here that guests are presented to The Queen during the many receptions held throughout the year.

LEFT

François Flameng (1856–1923), *Queen Alexandra*, 1908.

BELOW

Piano supplied by S. & P. Erard in 1856, in a gilded case decorated in eighteenth-century style by François Rochard (1798–1858). At Queen Victoria's request, the lid incorporates decorations from an earlier instrument supplied to the Queen in 1838.

MINISTERS' STAIRCASE AND MARBLE HALL

The Ministers' Staircase was introduced by Blore, providing alternative access to both the private and state rooms. The strict economy enforced on the completion of the Palace after the death of George IV is indicated by the balustrade, which was formed in gilt lead in place of the bronze used for the Grand Staircase. The wall opposite the landing was originally lit by a tall window, which at the end of Queen Victoria's reign was fitted with a stained-glass memorial to Prince Albert Victor (1864–92), the eldest son of Albert Edward, Prince of Wales.

BELOW LEFT
The Ministers' Staircase.

Lying directly below the Picture Gallery, the Marble Hall was originally designed for the display of sculpture. While suited in some ways to this purpose, lined with more of Joseph Browne's impressive columns and paved with coloured marbles, it was deficient in one crucial respect, namely natural light. The two sea-nymphs by Emil Wolff (1802–79) and Carl Steinhauser (1813–79) and the three works by Antonio Canova seen in the Marble Hall today were in fact displayed in the Picture Gallery and Silk Tapestry Room during the nineteenth century. Their plinths, in English alabaster and blue Hymettian marble, were designed by Frank Baines for those settings in 1915. The remainder of the sculptures now in the Marble Hall are further examples from the notable collection commissioned by Queen Victoria and Prince Albert from sculptors working in Rome. Like those in the Grand Hall, these were brought here from Osborne at King Edward VII's direction after 1902.

Apart from the columns, the floor and the two marble chimneypieces (which were removed from Carlton House), the decoration of the Marble Hall is fundamentally also the work of King Edward VII and his decorators. In the process, the gilt-wood swags and pendants of fruit and flowers were moved here from the East Wing.

BOW ROOM

This ample room was originally intended as a Library, at the centre of the suite of rooms on the ground floor that were to have served as George IV's private apartments. When the Palace was eventually occupied by Queen Victoria, these rooms were adapted to serve as drawing rooms for the newly reorganised Royal Household. The Bow Room was redecorated in 1853, the date included in the ceiling plasterwork, when it was used for the christening of Queen Victoria's youngest son, Prince Leopold (1853–84).

The Bow Room is now used on a daily basis as a waiting room for those being received in private audience by The Queen, in particular overseas diplomats presenting their credentials. It also serves as a dining room when The Queen entertains the

visiting head of state and their suite to lunch on the first day of a state visit. The Royal Family uses the room for lunches at Christmas and on special occasions, such as the 100th birthday of Queen Elizabeth The Queen Mother in 2000. The Bow Room forms part of the route from the Grand Entrance to the garden for the 30,000 guests who attend The Queen's garden parties each year.

ABOVE
Diplomats presenting their credentials to The Queen in the 1844 Room, which connects to the Bow Room.

LEFT
Part of the Chelsea porcelain 'Mecklenburg' service, made in 1763 for Queen Charlotte's brother, Duke Adolphus Frederick of Mecklenburg-Strelitz (1738–94); presented to Queen Elizabeth in 1947 by Mr James Oakes.

PALACE TIME

There are more than 350 clocks in Buckingham Palace, one of the largest collections of working clocks anywhere. Two full-time horological conservators wind them and keep them in good order.

ABOVE
Claude Galle (1759–1815), The 'Oath of the Horatii' clock, c.1800. Based on the famous 1794 painting by Jacques-Louis David (1748–1825), it was purchased by George IV in 1809. The story is from ancient Roman history and shows the three Horatii brothers receiving arms from their father, having sworn to fight for the supremacy of Rome.

LEFT
Alexander Cumming (1733–1814), Barograph, 1765. This barograph (a combination of a clock and a barometer) is one of the few objects in the state rooms to survive from George III's Buckingham House.

ABOVE
Pierre-Philippe Thomire (1751–1843), The 'Apollo' clock, early nineteenth century. Bought by George IV in 1810, it symbolises the passage of the sun through the sky, with the dial of the clock in the chariot wheel.

GARDEN

The 16-hectare garden forms part of an extraordinarily large and varied landscape at the heart of London, comprising St James's Park to the east and Green Park to the north. It is a reminder that Buckingham House, which George III purchased in 1762, lay right on the edge of the city of Westminster, and today it provides a habitat for 30 species of bird and over 350 species of wild flower. Nash, who had been much concerned with landscape design at Regent's Park and St James's Park, prepared the first designs for the laying out

LEFT
In the garden stand the Palladian temple, attributed to John Vardy (1718–65), and Richard Westmacott's Waterloo Vase. The vase was carved out of a single block of marble and weighs 20 tonnes.

BELOW
View of the Palace from across the lake.

RIGHT

Frederick Sargent
(fl. 1854–93), *The Garden
Party at Buckingham
Palace, 20 June 1887*,
1887–9.

OVERLEAF

The garden in the snow
with the West Front.
Over 73 metres in length,
the garden front remains
to some extent the
Palace's 'private' façade,
although it has long
formed the backdrop to
royal garden parties and
since 1993 has been part
of the public route.

of the new Palace garden in around 1825, but no concerted campaign of work was undertaken until after his dismissal in 1831. The man charged with its eventual completion was William Townsend Aiton (1766–1849), who had served George IV for many years in charge of royal gardens at Kew, Carlton House and Brighton and in 1827 was appointed 'Director of His Majesties Gardens'. It was Aiton who created the lake and the Mound, a high artificial bank on the southern side that screens the garden from the Royal Mews.

Today the garden is the setting for The Queen's three garden parties, which are usually held in July. During the rest of the year, the extensive lawns provide a landing site for The Queen's helicopter. In 2002, The Queen's two Golden Jubilee Concerts presented classical and pop music on separate nights, and took place in an unprecedented atmosphere of informality and celebration.

At the end of July each year, the tents for the service of tea and other refreshments and the temporary bandstand rapidly make way for the buildings erected for the use of summer visitors.

For the thousands of people who pass through Buckingham Palace each year, the state rooms and garden continue to represent the high standards of hospitality and extraordinary ceremonial that have characterised English royal palaces for centuries.

LEFT

The Queen and guests at
one of three annual
garden parties.